The Robot Scientist's Daughter

The Robot Scientist's Daughter

Poems by Jeannine Hall Gailey

Mayapple Press 2015

Published by   MAYAPPLE PRESS
                362 Chestnut Hill Road
                Woodstock, NY 12498
                www.mayapplepress.com

ISBN: 978-1-936419-42-5
Library of Congress Control Number: 2014943623

ACKNOWLEDGMENTS

The author gratefully acknowledges the journals and anthologies
where these poems first appeared:

*Archaeopteryx, Blue Lyra Review, Cerise Press, The Cincinnati Review,
The Cortland Review, Crab Orchard Review, Court Green, Eleven Eleven,
Escape Into Life, Fiction Southeast, 5 AM, Fourteen Hills, Illumen, The
Indiana Review, The 2013 Jack Straw Writer Anthology, The Journal, The
Los Angeles Review, MARGIE, Outside In Literary & Travel Magazine, The
Pedestal Magazine, Prairie Schooner, qarrtsiluni, Rattle, Redactions, The
Rumpus, The Skagit River Poetry Anthology 2014, Spoila, The 200 Poems
for New Mexico* web site.

Thanks to Two Sylvias Press for the use of "Chaos Theory" and
"The Taste of Rust in August," published in *She Returns to the Floating
World*.

"A Morning of Sunflowers (for Fukushima)" was selected as a $5,000
Dorothy Sargent Rosenberg award winner in 2011 and was published
among the winning poems on their web site.

Cover art by Masaaki Sasamoto. This is a combination of two images
from his COCORO series. Cover design by Judith Kerman. Text
design and layout by Amee Schmidt with titles in Baskerville Old
Face and text in Calisto MT.

Contents

III: You Can't Go Home Again

I would like to dedicate this book to my father, yes, a robotics professor and researcher, and to the people of Oak Ridge, Tennessee.

Author's Note

I grew up on a farm in Tennessee less than five miles downwind of Oak Ridge National Laboratories, where my father, who taught at the University of Tennessee, consulted on nuclear waste cleanup, specifically, robotics-based ways to clean up nuclear waste. The class issues inherent in setting up a sophisticated nuclear base in the middle of Appalachia were painfully clear to me as a child, but I loved growing up in Tennessee. It is still "home" to me more than any other place I've ever lived. Playing among deer and fishing streams with the Smokey Mountain backdrop, in a valley filled with flowers and fossils, was magical to me. Sadly, the two-story brick house, the steep banks covered with daffodils, fossil boulders that studded a yard with old-growth oaks above and moss and violets below, have all been paved over with concrete and abandoned—my mother's beloved lilacs and forsythia, my father's acres of strawberries, tomatoes and peas, a yard that was home to chickens, dogs, rabbits and horses. On Google maps, all that you can see of my old house and surrounding property is a flat, ugly, gray expanse. This book allows me to reanimate the landscape of my childhood.

But I also grew up in a house with a Geiger counter in the basement, various robots (including robot arms and chess-playing robots) and rows of books by Isaac Asimov and Ray Bradbury. I learned to program BASIC on a TRS-80 when I was seven. By high school and throughout college, I was helping my dad edit his papers on robotics and his consulting material on radioactive cleanup. There was never a time when I wasn't familiar with computers, robots and radioactivity. My first degree was a Bachelor of Science in Biology; I took a special interest in classes like ecotoxicology, medical botany, and even a class in "environmental law for engineers."

Oak Ridge National Laboratory was built in the middle of a heavily wooded area of the Tennessee Valley in the 1940's as part of the Manhattan Project. ORNL helped enrich uranium, and was the site of the creation of the first nuclear bomb dropped in Japan. After World War II was over, much additional research was done at ORNL, some of it safe, some of it, perhaps, not *as* safe. This picturesque wooded area west of Knoxville was also known as "The Atomic City," "America's Secret City," and a host of other ominous nicknames. (For additional fascinating vintage Americana pop culture expressing love of atomic science, there is nothing better than "Dagwood Splits the Atom," a comic made in the late 1940s, still available at the time of this writing: *http:// comicskingdom.com/blog/2012/10/10/ask-the-archivist-dagwood-splits-the-atom/*)

There were billboards and posters around the site warning those who worked there not to talk about their work, as well as threateningly-worded contracts for all who passed through their gates. Understandably, many former ORNL employees and contractors still don't say much about their work there, including my father. This means the stories, warnings and rumors about Oak Ridge tend to be hard to verify. Though the Tennessee citizens living around the facility tend towards the stoic rather than the fanciful, I grew up hearing the most amazing "ghost stories" about what really went on inside Buildings X, Y and K behind the ORNL gates, about glowing deer and radioactive catfish.

One reason I wrote this book was to raise awareness that nuclear research is never harmless; that the half-life of the pollution from nuclear sites is longer than most human lifespans; that there is, from reading my father's research as well as my college classes, no truly safe way to store nuclear waste. The devastation around Chernobyl and Fukushima is a reminder of the environmental, ethical and social costs of nuclear power. I've had lifelong health troubles, including autoimmune thyroid issues, which may or may not be linked to growing up in an area known for nuclear contamination.

I also wanted to tackle the pop culture representation of the atomic age, the depiction of scientists and their daughters in older sci-fi movies, and our attitudes towards science, particularly nuclear science. The fictional Robot Scientist's Daughter has many fantastic capabilities and experiences, but also shares many characteristics with me, and my fictional scientist is a conglomerate of historical figures like Oppenheimer, authors of books I read and yes, my father. This book is meant to be a gateway to a world of beautiful mutations and frightening flora, through the lens of our own culture's pop visions of the nuclear age.

I: Foxfire

Cesium Burns Blue

Copper burns green. Sodium yellow,
strontium red. Watch the flaming lights
that blaze across your skies, America—
there are burning satellites
even now being swallowed by your horizon,
the detritus of space programs long defunct,
the hollowed masterpieces of dead scientists.
Someone is lying on a grassy hill,
counting shooting stars,
wondering what happens
when they hit the ground.

In my back yard in Oak Ridge,
they lit cesium
to measure the glow.
Hold it in your hand:
foxfire, wormwood, glow worm.
Cesium lights the rain,
is absorbed in the skin,
unstable, unstable,
dancing away, ticking away
in bones, fingernails, brain.
Sick burns through, burns blue.

The Foxfire Books: In Case of Emergency, Learn to Make Glass

I remember burying acorns in the ground.
Sinister black hives housing nuclear bombs
built next door hovered over us. It seemed natural
that every day might be my last.

Nevertheless, there were violets to pick
from the moss by the oaks, there were dogs
and horses to stretch out next to, strawberries
to be gathered and smothered with sugar.

Each long sunbeam had its own message from God,
I was sure, hiding amidst the dust motes. I learned
the names of crawling creatures trapped, petrified,
in limestone rocks. I crawled inside abandoned bear caves
for shelter and tried to quiet my feet on the forest floor.

In case of poisoning, eat this. In case of war,
hide underground. I learned to purify water,
named edible leaves, in case, in case, in case.
It seemed as if the trees themselves were letting
in the light for me, as if I might lead people to safety.
I remember folding white sheets next to a Geiger counter.
Oil reserves burning up. It was the seventies.

My grandparents sent books of Appalachian rituals:
sassafras tea, planting peas by the moon, sewing up
the land. It seemed natural, then, that our woods
would grow glowing mushrooms, that it was the fire
of foxes, and we believed it could be appeased.

The Robot Scientist's Daughter [one of us]

There was something wrong with her; that much was clear.
She ran around in circles, meowing or mooing,
the yellowjackets a cloud in the sun. Men in black suits
hovered in doorways, dodging shadows; a safe was kept
locked at all times in her house.

The basement glowed and ticked, and the children
there emerged damaged. The furniture was cracked
and pasted back together—even the flowers in their blooms
knew soon they would be plowed under, left as rubble.
What chance did she have, even then? Did she know
how her future was already written, her roots stunted
and sick like those dogwoods with their grafted limbs?

Someone kept stealing their dogs, cars arrived in the night
and disappeared again before morning. Even though
their strawberries were so sweet, even though their daffodils
nodded cheerfully to us, we could see: she would never be
one of us.

Hot Wasp Nest

"Of the two kinds of wasps that built nests among the instru-ments, Shinn noticed that only the yellow-and-black daubers used radioactive mud."
       —Time, *August 1964, "Hot Wasps Nests"*

Slick with mud, the wasps' buzz punctuated afternoons
spent building nests that poisoned their young,
filling abandoned houses with the tick of radioactive dirt.

Poor wings, poor feet, unequipped but ambitious—
you didn't know the dosimeter, containment procedures,
only the whir of transfer, of architecture.

Swallows too, daubing the mud
on nests surely too fragile to protect
the chicks inside their eggs—

the scientists were following you as well,
to watch the spread of radionuclides,
project the radius of your flight.

O frog, O catfish, O white-tailed deer,
O invertebrate, O poisoned dears,
burn off, carry away, burrow underground.

14

Oak Ridge, Tennessee

We lived five miles downwind
of Oak Ridge National Labs.
Its towers contained multitudes.
My father's Geiger counter click-clicked
its swaying tongue at me.
Thirty years later, in the thyroids of local children—
cancers, syndromes, tumors.

(Dairy cows, asparagus and strawberry plants,
fruit in my mouth, snow in my hands.)

My mother was sprayed with pesticides as she played
in the fields as a child. My father grew up with pop guns
while men wrestled atoms. He learned to cap
contaminated soil with clay and concrete, their brittle grasp.

The reactor clasps graphite in a blank black building.
Here they built bombs, or the beginnings of bombs,
electricity crackling through the oak woods.
Once in the twenties, a madman, jailed
for prophesying the site, saying "here would be built…"
I don't know if he died in jail.
In my backyard, the skeletons of snails are trapped in lime.

(Red clay, lilacs, daffodils, black bears and mockingbirds.
Vines of honeysuckle and morning glory, children chewing
red clover.)

Always things hovering over us—mountains, thunderstorms…
a poisoned valley. Lightning bouncing across our yard.
Bees swarming a horse. My father strode off to work
with government-issue TLD cards and a black suit.
How much radiation today?
The card would tell him, but he knew it lied.

The Robot Scientist's Daughter [morbid]

is not as innocent as you think. Sure, she grieves
for the dead, for the destruction of even one baby rabbit
by a lawn mower, the kitten in the grass mauled
by dogs. She even saw her grandmother in a coffin,
still and beautiful with pink cheeks.
But her mother has started calling her morbid.

As a child she studied the Latin names for diseases,
the art of dissection, insisted upon the organization
of genus and species among her stuffed animals.
She had no problem pinning insects. This cannot end well,
her mother thought; she had encouraged playing
with other children, the joys of tag.

But instead the girl hides underground, pretending
to be a troll or a witch. She puts leaves in her hair
and collects fossils, lining them up to spell words,
the swirling trilobite, the imprints of the mysterious dead.

The Women of America's Secret City in 1945

*—Thanks to photographer Ed Westcott, whose photos
inspired this poem.*

Seated politely in plaid skirts and hot-rollered hair
at the controls of calutrons, having been warned
by a billboard on the way to work:

"What you see here...stays here."
Are told they have helped America win the war.
They are not yet concerned about uranium,

the cemestos (concrete and asbestos) walls
of their assigned rental homes,
the effects on their skinny children selling comic books

of "Atomic Men" for five cents on the side of the road.
A generation later, my father would walk these same buildings
with his dosimeter, talk to dying janitors, build robots

who might spare future janitors' lives. Design concrete caps
to protect us from decay. The women he worked with
every day were friendly, contained

like the particles under the K-25 and Y-12.
My childhood of barbed wire and warning signs
at the fishing holes, the simmer of the seventies,

protest versus patriotism, had none of that obedient beauty.
The horned-rimmed chemists and physicists
in sensible heels not questioning the yearly x-rays,
the uranium taped to their thin wrists.

The Taste of Rust in August

Knoxville afternoons in summer, lightning on the air.
The horses whinny, nervous; the chickens roost.

Our chain-link fence is rusty. I like to taste it—
that metallic clean I imagine to be the flavor

of lightning. My brother was hit once, carrying
a metal bucket to water the animals. It burned

his arm and left a funny taste in his mouth.
Mother says I have always sucked on spoons,

licked lampposts, iron grates, jewelry.
She goes crazy about the germs.

She says I do it because of what she calls *iron-poor blood*
and it's true—there's no rust in my skin at all,

dull and transparent as wax paper.
I run around the yard for hours, chasing the lightning,

tracing those fractal lines in the sky with my fingers
as the smell of ozone drives the dogs crazy.

The Robot Scientist's Daughter [villainess]

makes the perfect villainess. The impling can already
assemble solar coils and silicon chips, so make way.
In her hands a piece of paper becomes a bird,
a stack of metal a monster.

She grew up playing chess against the computer,
making aliens stick out their tongues.
She knows the click of the Geiger counter
better than her own heart, which moans
and swings unlike any machine.

She grew up with a string of undifferentiated dogs,
each slightly smarter than the last, each with its tongue
lolling to the side. They all looked exactly
like TV's Lassie, and they were all named Lassie.
We suspected them to be prototypes,
because of the spontaneous combustion.
There were always men in black,
always the clicking on the phone line,
and the badges we knew weren't to be trusted.

Like a game of chess, the making of bombs is delicate,
requires planning to assemble and disassemble.
What they sowed in the ground isn't gone;
it's in the mouths of their children when they chew
the weeds. Their children grow reedy
and anemic, their needy fists clenching,
skipping grades and affronting the public.
Any day now. We're watching.

The Girls Next Door

Lived in trailers and shacks that sagged over beams. Their floors were messy and their mothers smelled of old beer.

The girls next door taught me to curl my bangs, singeing earlobes and foreheads. They taught me to put on lipstick, pull a shirt down over my shoulder. Tuck a rose behind my ear. Cross my legs.

The girls next door were substitute sisters. I lived in a house full of boys.

The girls next door had parents who went to the hospital with knife wounds, gunshots to the stomach, bruises from frying pans. They never cried recounting these tales.

Their mothers yelled things like "I'm going to tear your arm off and beat you over the head with it" and I puzzled over how this would be accomplished.

Their mothers fed me, told me I was too skinny and pale. Sunshine and homemade brownies were remedies. They gave me clip-on earrings, slipped me five dollar bills for candy.

The girls next door had beautiful dark eyes, like Disney animals, long fringes of lashes.

The girls next door got pregnant too young. They moved far away from Knoxville. They became secretaries and real estate agents. They had children named after seasons and jewels: Autumn, Amber.

Lessons in Poison

I. Edible

She learned early to tell poison plants
because she liked to eat things in the yard—
wild onion, grass, green apples—to tell the fronds
of Queen Anne's Lace from hemlock, the snakeberry
from a strawberry, sassafras from poison oak,
that the prettiest mushrooms were the most toxic,
that lily of the valley and foxglove, though dainty,
were deadly.

But she didn't learn that the swallow's nest,
the frog, the mud-dauber wasp nest, the milk from cows,
the white-tailed deer, the catfish were full of hot particles.
Her father brought out the Geiger counter to measure
her snowmen and teach her the snow, too, wasn't
safe enough to taste.

II. Sassafras Tea

This was before she knew that this tea was carcinogenic, safrole illegal. But when she was little, she loved the five different leaves, like hand-imprints, the taste of the white twigs after she peeled away the bark. Her mother brewed the tea for her stomachaches, she would go into the woods and gather armfuls.

Some of the leaves looked like oak, some like poison ivy. They grew at a certain height, an eight-year-old child's height. White-tailed deer ate it, and mockingbirds. The smell sweet, effervescent as candy.

III. Foxfire

In the mountains, the blue light was called "foxfire." They said it was the lanterns of men lost in the forests, that it was ghosts or faery. In Oak Ridge National Labs, they found that radioactive Cesium put out a blue glow, made the metal look precious. This was before she learned about bioluminescence, about decaying molds on old leaves and deadwood, before she mixed chemicals in test tubes to create her own illumination.

The Robot Scientist's Daughter [medical wonder]

was a bit confused. She started down a road
to medical wonder, sat under the machine's lights,
but then tiptoed off on a paper trail,
looking for an island of cranes. She made a thousand
wishes; still she shed a blue glow and everyone said
how sickly. Her nails made of plastic and paper maché,
her heart's thump-thump three times too fast.
Her one kidney curled inside her ribs, her blood trying
to escape. *"Father!"* she screamed, but he couldn't save her.

The robot scientist's daughter knew what she had to do.
With her own two hands she built a new body, one
that worked better this time, silver and shiny and smooth
as mirrored glass. After all, she'd been trained,
it was no less than was expected. She crawled inside
and adjusted the fit. This time, there will be no stopping
her. The curves are all impenetrable, and the precision
of each drum-kit-beat keeps her in line. She's a soldier,
a savior, a ship to bear prisoners into space.

The Robot Scientist's Daughter [Before]

This was back when she still made birds' nests
with mud and twigs, hoping that birds would
come live in them. She placed them in the crooks
of maple, apple and pear trees, waiting patiently
for them to lay eggs. Her skin was covered in insect bites
and scratches from scrambling over shale and rough bark,
her hair long and tangled.

She wanted to imitate the mockingbird, learned to whistle
for mourning doves. She hid in the honeysuckle
and crept up quietly on foxes and even sometimes
small bears. She still believed she could talk to animals.
She wasn't afraid then of anything, not the biggest
roaming dogs or the yellowjackets, yet. She prayed
to become one of them—the birds fluttering the leaves,
the cats whose fur she pressed her face into, a wolf
or a jaguar. This was back when she still believed in prayer.

She hid underneath the wide shadows of leaves.
She lay in the moss and broke violet stems with her fingers,
brought the violets and mosses indoors, where they wilted.
This was before she became afraid of light.

II: Aberrations

How Not to Be a Robot Scientist's Daughter

Stay away from Nevada, New Mexico, Hanford, Oak Ridge. From remote areas with good water circulation away from prying eyes.

Never go looking in your father's closets. In the basement. In the laboratory. Don't open, don't spin. Don't adjust the settings. Don't touch the box marked "U."

When you finish your first computer class at seven, don't wave your certificate proudly. Don't beg for your mother not to leave your father. Don't cry in the car holding your heavy disc in your fist.

Don't fall in love with the flowers—they are transient. You do not realize it now. Every hour you spend with them is wasted.

Don't trust the green screen, the blue glow. Never let your fingers learn the keyboard by heart.

Don't spend hours at Radio Shack, picking out gifts your father wants you to have—a built-your-own-radio kit, a robotic car, one tiny machine after another. He will give away your robotic toys. When you ask to whom, he will say "kids who needed them more than you."

When you grow up, don't emulate your father's tethered temper, your mother's quickness with figures. Don't try to fuse their troubled tensions, his lack of words, her impatience with broken circuitry.

When you are the robot scientist's daughter, they open you up and find a mass of wires instead of a heart, your neural networks nothing but artificial intelligence, but this surprises no one. Don't reveal your bionic nature.

Iodine-131

in our rainwater, months later the ions
gather in our forests, the drops on our lips
as we watch the heron and otter in the river.

We don't fear what we can't see.
Like the schoolchildren in Yokohama
fed beef from radioactive cows,

we continue to play in the dirt, unaware
and uncaring. Our vocabulary lesson:
becquerels per liter, beta decay.

Today the children pick flowers. Our friend
submits his arm to a needle of vinchristine,
extract of Madagascar periwinkle, to kill cancer cells

gone mad inside him. Our mitosis ceases,
a danger, our life-cycles interrupted with rainwater,
with fish and grass we cannot know completely.

Oak Ridge is a Mystery

It cannot be penetrated because the dark leaves
of the trees stand so close together you can hear
them whisper, "Keep out." The carpet of needles
beneath your feet, silencing. The foxfire in the woods
an illusion of light, the mountains hung with
a shroud of smoke.

The robot scientist is a mystery to his daughter,
a cipher that cannot be explicated. His badge is magical.
The clicking of his lab equipment warns her, "Keep Out."
Even now they rely on the whisk of data packets
on high-speed cable as a way to tell the truth.
Computers don't lie; they only do what they are told.
Your secrets are safe with them.

Oak Ridge National Labs is a mystery, so many signs
saying "Keep Out." So many files have been labeled
"Confidential: To be opened…" Our physicist tour guide
laughs, jokes around as he leads us through Buildings
X, Y and K; but you know what he can't say,
what he whispered into closed files.

Oak Ridge is a mystery; the dark place in the earth
where poisons are buried, where the worms do their work.
How the grass raises its head even though it carries
a heavy metallurgical load. How the trout and catfish tackle
the brooks down the hillside stacked with mud. The wings
of the wasp and the swallow whirring: Keep Out.

America Dreams of Roswell

The forbidding sugar of hot desert sand
and hallucinations of mushroom clouds

linger in a city where you can still get pie
with a fried egg on top, where you might catch

a glimpse of UFO dazzle, even the lampposts bloom
into alien heads, where barbed wire might keep out enemies

of the American dream, where the tiny famous lizard's legs
cling to sad, solid rock. On the Trinity site, that sand

turned to green glass. The scientists were unsure
about igniting the whole earth's atmosphere, nevertheless

the violet light demanded goggles; the shadows
of ranch houses burned into the ground.

Chaos Theory

Elbow-deep in the guts of tomatoes,
I hunted genes, pulling strand from strand.
DNA patterns bloomed like frost. Ordering
chaos was my father's talisman; he hated
imprecision, how in language the word
is never exactly the thing itself.

He told us about the garden of the janitor
at the Fernald Superfund site, where mutations burgeoned
in the soil like fractal branchings. The dahlias and tomatoes
 he showed to my father, doubling and tripling in size
and variety, magentas, pinks and reds so bright
they blinded, churning offspring gigantic and marvelous
from that ground sick with uranium. The janitor smiled
proudly. My father nodded, unable to translate
for him the meaning of all this unnatural beauty.

In his mind he watched the man's DNA unraveling,
patching itself together again with wobbling sentry
enzymes. When my father brought this story home,
he never mentioned the janitor's slow death from radiation
poisoning, only those roses, those tomatoes.

The Robot Scientist's Daughter [in films]

is always beautiful in films, in a neat blonde updo
and fifties-style dress. She helps the hero escape.
She leads him off the island or planet,
she gives him the code to shut down all the robots
before they take over the world. The robot scientist's
daughter carefully holds on to secrets
about her father at the dinner table. She's demure
but knows her way around a gun rack or a test tube.
She sneaks out to rescue prisoners after her father
has a drink. The robot scientist's daughter must be there
to humanize the robot scientist; he is both a protagonist
we identify with and a villain we know must fall.
If he had no daughter, the camera would have no way
to enter his laboratory with a sympathetic eye.
Sometimes the robot scientist's daughter pretends to be
a robot herself, handing out food efficiently without
smudging her makeup. Sometimes she turns out
to be a robot all along, implanted with heartwarming
but false memories. Sometimes she has a telepathic link
to genetically-engineered dinosaurs. When she was a child,
she had only robots to play games with, mostly hide-and-seek
and chess. This helped and hurt her socialization.
The robot scientist might be named Morbius,
while his daughter is named Susan. She will be
the downfall, the island crumbling, scientist buried
beneath rubble, killer shrews loosed on the world.

The Robot Scientist's Daughter [tinkering]

Like a robot, she keeps dislocating joints,
must be recalibrated, adjusted, attuned
carefully to weather conditions.

The chemistry must be tested: more alkaline,
more acid. Lithium ions in the 7-Up.
Cesium in the sunflowers.

Unexplained fatigue, scan for system failures
sparked by magnetic waves. Plans for extended
warranties, spare parts

when one or another breaks down. Altered past
recognition, we're playing games with genomes.
Was I planted in a test tube, born in a sterile

laboratory? They all cried: It's alive!
Against all odds, the lightning bolt
charged the helpless heart, the iron lung

and steel plates aligned. Calcium, magnesium,
nitrates, poisons and pollutants:
that's what little girls are made of.

Raised in a nuclear city, under leaden skies,
her wandering hands grasping the dirt,
as if to return, as if to say, this is where I belong.

She Explains Her Fear of Bees

I am seven, my little brother is four. He is riding a pony in the front yard. It's a beautiful day; his blonde hair makes a halo in the sunshine. I lie in the grass in the cool shade of oak trees. My parents are elsewhere.

The pony steps on a yellow jacket hive hidden underground. They swarm boy and pony so quickly with a sound like the earth growling. I scream. The pony rolls to the ground to crush the bees, my brother still in the saddle. He is light and tossed aside, but swollen with stingers.

There are over sixty bee stings in pony and brother; I count them with my fingers. Someone carries him indoors…

You ask me why I jump when I hear bees. Why they carry such menace. My little brother lying on the couch, packed in ice and antihistamines. Those bees so angry on a summer day, the innocent damage of a horse's hoof, the stillness of shadow broken, my fragile brother so close to the brink

of something irrevocable I didn't yet understand. Yellow jackets don't lose their stinger, like honeybees. They keep stinging. They are really wasps, not bees at all, little liars. Why do they hide underground? To teach us dangers unseen—to watch our step, to protect, to cover, to dodge.

Knoxville, 1979

It is late spring, I am on my knees
pulling peanuts out of the red dirt.
I shake the thin fibrous stalks, like spider webs,
and when I put them in my mouth they taste
like metal. I like the scrape of them against my teeth.

The hum of the lawn mower grows louder
in the afternoon. My father puts me on his lap
and lets me drive it. Sometimes when my parents
aren't watching I eat the grass too,
like I am a horse or lawn mower. The grass tastes green
and snaps like onion.

We retreat from the rain that soaks the clay ground
at sundown. We boil the peanuts and rhubarb. The steam
fills the kitchen with tart, salt scents.

Those peanuts, with their frayed roots holding loosely
to the hostile soil that yields rust, rust,
with threads so close to breaking.

Multiple Chemical Sensitivity

It began with eating grass. Later, she grew welts
where she used soap. Once, what fell from the sky
was clean; once, there was no brown layer

over the valleys. Everything she touches feels like fire;
her skin puckers and reddens when she does her hair
or cleans the sink. The skin has a semi-permeable

membrane, she learned in school, each cell, too.
She was tired, she ran a fever and struggled to breathe.
She felt like running away, but where could she run

that her own body wouldn't betray her, wouldn't react,
wouldn't try to push the poisons out?
She felt herself ticking off the elements in the body:

oxygen, carbon, hydrogen, nitrogen, fluorine,
sulfur, strontium, mercury. How many elements
can be lit on fire? What color does the body burn?

She herself would be blue and green, she thought,
like glass. She dreams about a toxic forest, about cells
that grow long and fibrous, about poisonous spores.

If the water and earth are contaminated,
the trees and mushrooms try to absorb it,
the fruit itself becomes poison. Fifty years ago,

they set off bomb after bomb in the desert,
setting mushrooms of smoke across the sky,
annihilating wasp and yucca plant and tiny

jewel-like lizard. They did not think of fallout.
They did not think of anything but the clap
of thunder, the blazing blue light they had made.

The Robot Scientist's Daughter [triangulate]

woke up and didn't know   which way to go.

A waiting game,   a holding pattern,

a killdeer triangulating sound in the sands.

On one hand, a predator.

    On the other, a pair of stockings.

The Robot Scientist's Daughter [circuits]

is good with circuits, the diagrams laid out like pin-up girls.
She knows the beauties of voltmeter and oscilloscope.
She couldn't help but put the wires right. Her own wiring
was off, though—she touches the tip of her tongue
to a balloon for the electric shock, her hair standing out
in points. You never knew what would set her going.
Sparks vibrate from her fingers and vocal chords.

The Robot Scientist Considers Asimov's First Law

The Robot Scientist sits alone in a room encased in glass,
examining a robot arm that crushed someone to death
in a factory. He thinks it is not the robot's fault.
He feels sympathy for the robot, who only does
what it is told. So much of the Robot Scientist's life
is spent in rooms trying to solve problems
involving wires and networks. When he was younger
he had more energy for the problems; he tried
to figure out the problems of his wife
and daughter in the same way, the wrong wiring,
the crossed signal. The arm going haywire, the man
holding his crushed skull, the blood on the cold blue floor.
The robot was just obeying orders, following the lines
drawn on concrete. The Robot Scientist must go
before a jury, say the robot was just following procedures.
The man holding his skull. The crossed wires.
So many broken arms.

Elemental

The titanium staple
the surgeon left in your stomach
is just the beginning:

it's the strontium-90 in your baby teeth,
in the bones of your parents.
(The dust of New Mexico, the echoes of
tests of implosion triggers
fifty, sixty years ago.)

Note the Americium in your smoke detector.
Note the rate of decay per second.
The trees drink Cesium click click click
The bees weave particles into their nests click click click

The traces around you
of other people's experiments
linger in your veins, lungs, eggs
linger in your femur and kidney.

Carbon-based structures,
we absorb from the water, from the air,
from our food, from our walls
from our parks and fishing ponds.

We absorb and our body says:
it is good.

The Scientist

For K.Z.M.

Lives alone in a house made of snow.
If he makes music, no one hears it.
He engineers the splitting of atoms,
the splitting of wires, the splitting of hearts.
The spit of handmade radio wire. And never
any connection. The scientist cannot take responsibility
for the laws of physics, even for his own children,
the degradation of molecules under the microscope.
Did he cause that cloud over the city?

It's unthinkable that his hands, his theories,
hidden away now in notebooks…That's what
he tells himself, that he taped uranium to the wrists
of nurses to see if it burned, that he tested and watched
them die. He forgets, he grows older. He writes
about the beauty of the storm, the lumen of Cesium
alight with blue flame.

"Fukushima Mutant Butterflies Spark Fear"

—Title taken from a news headline on Twitter in 2012

Blue grass butterflies born eyeless
wings misshapen, legs hapless
bring doubts, invite speculation
whisper: cancer, mutation, third generation

like a butterfly wing's path on the skin
each unravelling molecule
blossoms into its own miraculous monster
don't wait for the poisonous wind

or the downstream effects
under the ground our monsters sleep
and form poisons inside us, curling our fingers
graying our hair, forming tumors quietly in the night.

The Robot Scientist's Daughter [director or dictator]

knew she was meant for better things,
but couldn't marshal the resources. More specifically:
other people did what she told them,
but not her own body, a traitorous animal
that squirmed out of her grasp.
She put herself in the right places
in the right clothes and opened her mouth.
Of course, all that came out was song.

Her teachers all told her that she, like Barbie,
could be President—but the President of what?
She knew she was a mutant, unlike
her three brothers who were all lost in the woods
(on occasion she drew them back to the house
with gingerbread.) They were all hale and hearty
while she grew paler after each sunset.
They flew off honking like swans leaving her
alone to weave their shirts for them, give them back
their voices. Anyway, looking around her,
she was happy with the apple blossoms,
happy with her skin fine and translucent as sea glass,
happy even when her lungs hurt and her blood pooled
because being alive is a kind of happiness.
She embraced her own atoms: she told them,
"Now behave this way, not that way, I am not
ready to lose you." She was told to lead armies,
could not make her own sentry enzymes stand guard,
could not keep tumors from multiplying, could not form
her own entrails into something symmetrical to read
like a prophesy. She was a frustrated dictator or director,
fit only to spin stories—she knew she should lean into the ears
of children, whisper to them fantastic lies, send them out
into the universe knowing they had control
of everything, everything, their own sick demented
molecules and the way they would plow through the world.

Death by Drowning

It is my first memory. I am three. My parents
are elsewhere, watching the new baby, the computer
screen. The world is blue and I cannot get air
into my lungs. All around me is cold chlorine and alien
aqua. It has been one minute.

One minute I was walking with warm grass beneath
my bare feet, the next my feet touched the surface
of what looked like glass, and I was under. I cannot float,
merely thrash six feet underwater. If only I was a smooth
sleek seal, a dolphin, a mermaid, if only vestigial gills
might open. It has been two minutes.

I have forgotten my own name, my parents. When an arm
finally reaches down to me, it is my brother's.
He is shouting at me, won't stop shouting. *Her lips
are blue, she's not breathing, do something.*

I try to do something. The chlorine scratches at my eyes
and alveoli. I have not yet started to breathe. I am three
and have not yet started coughing, trying to expunge
the memory of chemical water from my lungs, have not yet
learned the fear of water.

The Robot Scientist's Daughter [the other]

was often mistaken for a vampire or a Mormon.
She was allergic to the sun, to alcohol, to garlic.
And all that blood—every nosebleed was a spectacle.
You had to expect the whispering of the villagers,
the insistence on burning. You had to expect the knock-
knock on the door in the middle of the night,
the exchange of paperwork. Her mother handing
her over to strangers who stuck her with needles.
Later she studied fashion magazines to look more
like the others. No more ruffles, no more black cloaks.

Change your shoes, change your life! crowed the headlines.
She wondered if it were true. Still, the flashes of white
at her neck and hands were telling. Are you Russian?
asked a man. French? They all accused her of being
a "foreigner," a "changeling." It was true she did not
chew gum or tan. It was true she kept scraps of paper
in her pockets and hair. She learned blankness of spirit,
hoped they would ignore the telltale signs.

Radon Daughters

are invisible and odorless. They float in air
for a few minutes, then like to attach to other particles:
dust, smoke, mist.

The general population has been exposed
to these isotope offspring—polonium, lead, bismuth.
The radon daughters lurk in lungs, biding their time.

They sing: decay, father Radon, decay into a fine spray,
so fine we will be inhaled into lungs, carried away
to alveoli, snapping, twinkling, emitting the sharp
tack-tack of the alpha particle.

We are short-lived, unstable, airborne,
three unattached daughters
longing for the cyclone of breath.

The Robot Scientist's Daughter [experiments in sleep deprivation]

They believed she was designed to be a supersoldier.
They used a CT scan to look for infiltrants
to her heart and lungs. They kept her up all night
with lights and sirens to test her will.
When she nodded off, they prodded her with needles.

She's forgotten the lessons of mushrooms, of mongrels,
of her childhood. In fact, she can't even remember running.
Is it possible it was all a dream? Now the grim facts
march before her: another enemy body part rebelling,
another tamping down of her own systems in order to observe
and operate. They try to tamper and tame her piece by piece.

In her dreams they are telling her about fluid
in the lungs. They ask her if she would rather be
Margaret Atwood or Sylvia Plath. Louise Glück,
she answers without thinking, because of the fabulous shoes. Now
there was a woman who knew how to garden,
she talked with the flowers, knew how to shop for cheese.
An enviable, contained life, as precise as the X-Acto knife
her father invented. The daughters of inventors are bound
to circumscribe their father's creations with words.

In twenty days she has not slept the night.
They think it's impossible to hold her.
She throws the machines into mystification.
They cannot pin her down, not yet.
She resists the urge to sing.

The Robot Scientist's Daughter [sign of hope]

always had a metallic taste in her mouth.
Maybe it was from the soil, the grass
she had eaten as a child playing horse.
Perhaps it was the time she put her tongue
on the spark plugs. It turned everything bright and sharp:
potato chips, pasta. In her recipes, sugar and salt
were used interchangeably. She distrusted candy
that melted into air, spun sugar and puffed mint balls.
She preferred products of the earth: raw peanuts,
slightly wooden pears. She met a man who fixed her
plates of fragrant produce. She could practically
hear the cell walls bursting. She put him under
the microscope, and even his molecules
were blond and even. She tied herself to him,
and he built trinkets out of the rope.
In return she drew a circuit in which she directed energy
in parallel lines. This was a sign of hope.

III: You Can't Go Home Again

A Morning of Sunflowers (for Fukushima)

Two hundred thousand sunflowers
drink the cesium from the grounds of the temple
where they burn the names of the dead.

This invisible snow, says the temple's monk,
brings us a long winter. A village woman mourns
the loss of her blueberries.

In Chernobyl they grew amaranthus, field mustard,
sunflowers. But how to dispose
of poisoned flowers in spring?

We build lanterns. We plant seeds. We set things alight.

The Robot Scientist's Daughter [apocalyptic]

has always been enamored of apocalypse.
On television screens, when the mushroom
clouds bloomed. In books, as layer by layer
of humanity is peeled away. The disasters laid out
in newspapers. She loves the way a dinosaur's face
on the page looks like it might be sleeping, dead
thousands and thousands of years. She dreams
of thunderclouds, meteor strikes and nuclear bombs.
Her mother tells her, in the old days they had concrete
bomb shelters. To her they sound wonderful, like magic
islands of canned food and Jell-O. She knows about radiation;
there's no safe dose. She knows her father measures it
each day when he goes into work. She doesn't know yet
about the birthing of bombs, doesn't realize yet
the way destruction is crafted, like a work of art.
She thinks the explosions are beautiful;
she still thinks the snow piling around her is safe.

Oak Ridge National Laboratory: Unlock the Secrets of America's Secret City!

You read, *it's only dangerous for children who drank the milk, who ate the produce.* Pears and apples, asparagus and peanuts, rows and rows of lettuce, the eggs from chickens you raised by hand. Snow cones. Milk shakes. Homemade ice cream with blackberries and rhubarb.

Unbelieving, you point out your address: 710 Mabry Hood Road. They've razed it. Now all that's left are puzzle pieces of cement where the foundation was laid. They meant to put up a psychiatric hospital, but abandoned those plans and now, although that mangled rose garden is gone, you still can find your fossil rock, where you hid in the shadows of trees.

Your neighbors' ramshackle shack still stands, though your neighbors (the wife who stabbed her husband, their sons who brought you crates of stolen mangoes) have disappeared. They never trusted the government men, with their dark suits, their mysterious questions.

You remember the dogs—the sheltie that was stolen, lolling with collie dogs, the sad beagle puppies. The bear that lived in the woods you thought you heard when you were hiking. The mockingbirds you tried to imitate in the morning, your hands pulling at the tough vines of honeysuckle and morning glory. You remember fishing, trout and bass pulling at the corn on your line.

The soft spring sky still lolls above ghosts of your old home, seems to forgive the dank basement its crimes, the orange-and-avocado kitchen, now rubble. And still, fields where strawberries grew yield them unevenly.

You drive past Oak Ridge, down Kingston Pike lined with white churches. You drive past one hundred Cracker Barrels, Ruby Falls, Cade's Cove, green cool stretches like the wings of green birds, rising irretrievable.

Tickling the Dragon

For Louis Slotin

About suffering they were never wrong, the old comics:
Dr. Manhattan's accident a perfect recreation of Slotin's,
poisoned before his frightened co-worker's eyes.
Here's the drawing of him holding his screwdriver,
tickling the dragon. Oppenheimer would complain
about his pangs of conscience, the images of his friend
haunting him. They could imagine what he described:
the sour taste in his mouth, the pain in his hand.
They could still see that blue glow around him,
feel the heat wave from beryllium meeting plutonium
core. His retching, then nine days of futile blood
transfusions. "A bomb putter-togetherer," he called
himself, though the bomb would take him apart
atom by atom. After this, they began to use robots;
they wanted to find a way to keep a man's hands
from touching the demon core of this dragon.

Phosphorous Girl

is the shadow in white dust you left behind.

I imagine she either went off with a jazz musician
or followed her dream of veterinary school
somewhere in the Midwest. She dresses in discarded
prom dresses and dances around to Psychedelic Furs.

White phosphate hidden in her bones, she ignites
the paper caps in cap guns and snaps her fingers
like she's striking a match.

She believes she was poisoned by radiant steam;
she believes her bones were burned
by GMO corn and Roundup-infused grass.

She dreams of *Akira* and Chernobyl as she sleeps
by slow rivers that run with fertilizer and green shampoo.

The Robot Scientist's Daughter [Polonium-210]

is a tightly-controlled molecule.
Sometimes she threatens
to explode into antimatter,
to shatter the equilibrium.
Other times she teeters
at the edge of decay, a half-life
of skin and soul. Shake her if you will:
you don't want to stand too close.
She is extremely unstable. She is toxic;
inhaling or consumption can lead to death.
She is considered fairly volatile.
She can be contained within paper.
She glows bright blue. She is a showstopper.

"Now I Am Become Death"

—J. Robert Oppenheimer, scientific director of the Manhattan
Project, quoting from the Bhagavad Gita

Flying machines and exploding atoms,
you sure made our dreams come true.
You're standing at the blackboard,
and from here your physics looks good
but the math just awful. You are the destroyer
of worlds, just like you told us, dragging
behind you sad bodies of monsters in the sand,
your children, their teeth and bones rattling,
wailing piteously. Oh pray for us, father of bombs,
Opje, Oppie, pray for this new future
where you've planted plutonium among tulips,
polonium in the desert, cesium in the cow's milk.
Pray for these mutant fingers, typing in the last days,
for lips that spit out your name like a curse.

The Scientist Solves a Puzzle

Like the boy in the Snow Queen story,
playing with ice and fire, trying to spell
"love" or "salvation," ending up with only broken
shards. I don't remember what I wanted
to accomplish. When did I find myself so far away,
so bruised with frost, so unseeing? There are crystals
in my heart, fragments of mirror in my eye.
I stack one atom next to another, then force them
apart, race them against the clock. I'm only guessing.
Endothermic, exothermic. Is that what brought on this
nuclear winter? I forget. I remember a long time ago
I thought it would always be exciting, that logic
would save the day, man's triumph over matter.
White lab coats, secret caves for experiments.
Atomic man. Radioactive boy. Tick tick tick.

The Robot Scientist's Daughter [ghost in the machine]

is reincarnated, this time as a machine who believes
she is human. She is perfect, full of light and joy
she never knew when she was merely flesh.
The world around her hums with unknowable rhythms;
the sunshine reflected off rooftops after rain, the quacking
of ducks, the cars that zoom past each other on the freeway.
She does not ask questions anymore; instead, she prays,
and instantly receives answers programmed in ones
and zeroes. The new, less-human version recognizes
her good luck, recognizes the green grass as a gift
that quickly withers. Her hand is light on your arm,
her eyes still the color of the sea, the color of the silver gears
inside her head. We wonder where she will go,
this miracle, this marvel, whether she will go on
to be an astronaut or environmental engineer.
This time she believes anything is possible; there is no
resistance from the feeble guts, the slow, ponderous breath.
Her tongue is alive with lasers and her song attracts
thousands. She will stop bullets with her steel skin.
She will breathe new life into the species.

On the Night of a Lunar Eclipse, a Missile Shoots Down a Spy Satellite

Unstable frozen fuel tank *deadly hydrazine gas*
with the impact of a 1000 pound bomb
the size of two football fields.

minimize risk to terrestrial areas

coma seizure burned lungs burned skin

The cleanup mission labeled "Burnt Frost"
waiting in my city, trucks and decontamination
suits at the ready.

On that night the moon, as dark and red as the mottled face
of an angry man waving his gun in the face of another,
hides from us, gives us back our shadow
and in that shadow we see the stars.
It would take minutes they said
to burn the lungs enough to kill…

even if you survive inhalation
your kidneys, thyroid, liver, brain

And the sea so quiet, ready to accept one more gift
from us, one more handful of debris on the trajectory
my home and yours.

unstable weather conditions make it hard to predict
uneven land masses *population density*
football fields

What's raining from the skies isn't love.
The sky is falling the news headlines read.
The moon has turned from us and dimmed.

The war ships force their spacecraft homeward
in shards, one more failed seeker
with a heart of metal and poison.

The Robot Scientist's Daughter [nomad]

is a nomad who roams the streets looking for evidence
of God. Around her the crashed debris of society.
She lists the scientific names of butterflies: Lepidoptera,
Nymphalidae. In every town, the freeways are the same
but the weather patterns shift; one day dense fog,
the next, tornadoes in an empty gold field.

The road unwraps like scissors slicing down a strip
of ribbon to make it curl. American towns melt into
sunsets, into dust clouds, into faces friendly and
unfriendly. She spent her childhood meandering
from frozen New England towns to the sunny smogs
of Southern California, her father always in search
of something, a better life; her mother making do,
not asking questions. She remembers her eyes full of tears
and her fist full of cupcake, one of her earliest memories
saying *goodbye, goodbye* from a moving car.

Like Monarch butterflies on their archaic march,
or hummingbirds filling their bellies for flight
from Canada to Mexico, she has taken wing,
soaring from one continent to another, a great
migration leaving only the barest hint of her struggles
behind. Some say there was a sighting in New Haven,
or maybe Tennessee. You should know she's careful
to leave no signs for predators.

The Robot Scientist's Daughter [escape]

was an escape artist. She'd watched her father x-ray
roses and peonies, knew the ins and outs
of the genome. Each city collapsed under her gaze;
ice-storms in the desert, drought among the bananas.
The newspapers blared the news, but she was already gone.
Sometimes she brought souvenirs—a café from Cuba
plunked down in Sweden, a spun-sugar swan at the seaside.
No one understood the apparitions.

She loved shadow-puppets. Her hands became doves,
cranes, foxes. But these were messages. Inside she itched
to be set free. She ran in caves underground. She thought
the green glow was the same, that somehow the crickets
could communicate, the stalactites soothe her skin.
On the tops of mountains, she communed with planets,
swinging the earth dangerously close to the sunspots,
knocking comets out of orbit. She thought when she sang
the seals could understand, with their soft eyes, unwieldy
bodies. She swam in the sea, in black currents and red tide.
She thought she might be a mermaid, with her seaweed hair
and strange labored lungs. She sang and sang but no one
heard. There is a rattling of undersea earthquakes.
She might move the moon closer for company.

She Introduces Her Husband to Knoxville

First, the green highway with big white churches,
then, new roadway paved with dollars from ORNL,
the dilapidated houses sagging along the road, rusted
cars up on blocks, the children running with dirty mouths.
The daffodils nod in clumps, the occasional fox darts
in the road. She directs him to Mabry Hood Road,
the blank canvas that was once her yard, her house,
the gardens carefully tended for sixty years.

Spirea, forsythia, then lilac or japonica, the wild stems
of crepe myrtle, the tulip magnolia, and here was where
the pink dogwood bloomed, the one with the grafted
branches. Here was the driveway she had learned to ride
a bike on, where her brother's motorcycles had spun
angrily on gravel. Here, touch this: here was her fossil
rock, like a tooth-root unmovable

in the bare dirt. And the strawberries: nothing grows.
The red clay bleached by years. He asks her to imagine,
one last time, the sun's glow on the screen door after rain,
the lily-of-the-valley and foxglove gathered in her tiny fists,
the acorns she planted, the shells of cicadas,
the half-wild dogs around her legs as she learned to climb
the maple and pear trees. Her first snow. She tells him there's
nothing to see here.

Advice from the Robot Scientist's Daughter

After all, the moon has fallen asleep and you are alone.
Try to see with my vision: the breaking of membrane,
the fragile fruit withering, embryos curling within eggs.
Living beings so friable, so prone to overgrowth
and imbalance. Organic and inorganic: inside the rose petal,
a blue skeleton. Remember, after all, that we can incinerate
or incubate; that your atoms right now are smashing against
the atoms of your chair. What is keeping you together?
The pull of the moon, the arms of a lover, the gravity
of cherry to cherry stone. Keep from being broken apart.
Keep things from being broken apart. Gather together:
thyroid, womb, heart. Build a nest. How can we avoid
the rays that, right now, seek to destroy at a molecular level? Now
I understand the sea, the great embrace, water and light moving in
a wave formation. Keeping it all together.

The Robot Scientist's Daughter Journeys West

She's a bit of an alien here in the land
of tanned legs and blonde hair, beaches
and bongo drums, but she waves with delight
at the seals sunning themselves on the rocks.
What a long journey, leaving skins and false limbs
in her path, not in a covered wagon but all the same
she reins it in. Once over the mountains, she could see
the flower fields on all sides, the winding and happy light
on bare shoulders. So what if the crispy trees were devoured every
so often by fire, or the hills slid down in the rain,
if the earth rattled a little along the fault lines? In a land
of cartoon mice you learn not to question; besides, she felt
she was born to Imagineer. The books were so clean here, hardly
touched at all, and the air smelled of funnel cake.

The Robot Scientist's Daughter [recumbent]

She lies back on a floor of pine needles looking up at a sky
obscured by crooked branches. But she can't be back—
this must be memory, tricking her, her hands on the damp
violets and moss, the sharp shells of acorns a mirage.
If she could, she would once again be part of this wood,
her own cells the building blocks of the next flower,
the next kit fox. Trace elements still exist inside her
that call her to this place, the skeleton of decayed leaves
a reminder that her own skeleton, marrow emptied out,
might emit the same markers, might show
the exact same chemical makeup. When she was young
there were so many daffodils, she could not pick them all—
she ran her hands along their frilled faces, she placed
her face in their clusters and smiled, covered in yellow
pollen. Even the glue of their stems on her hands smelled
like sunshine. One more trick. She lies back,
and remembers perennials that no longer exist.
She will not die here in concrete. Her body belongs there,
in a flower-field tilled under, waiting, vast and empty,
for her to return.

For the Robot Scientist: Questions of Fission and Fusion

When you majored in nuclear physics you thought you could save—

When you visited the janitor's garden the flowers so futile, so fragrant, exploding with double and triple petals, the janitor's bones and blood, the rate of decay—

When you learned about the algae and the bamboo, the way that radiation glowed in the cells of trees—

When you read to us, Meg and Charles Wallace saved their father and the world in L'Engle's snowy apocalyptic landscape, the evil a hot wind beating its wings.

In our backyard, squirrels and catfish, little garter snakes in my hand, the nests of birds, little poisoned eggs…the swallows tracked, and those mud-daubers.

When you studied the periodic table, you learned about the half-lives, the incredible slow decay, the inexorable tick-tock of a watch set for centuries.

When you studied CT scans and MRIs, when you took mammograms of roses and hung them on our wall, the skeletons so fragile, so blue, like all of us, a reminder.

When you studied electrons breaking apart, did you want them to hold together like a family with a secret, the center force spinning us farther out?

Fukushima in Fall: A Field of Sunflowers

grows where rice should stand, to draw cesium
from the earth. The water lilies bloom
after years of lying dormant. Something here about

the resilience of earth, of humanity; something hopeful
in the faces of those yellow sunflowers, turning towards
the last beams of light. Children hesitate before tasting
plum jam, before sipping tea:

how can they know what is offered? And everyone says
it is safe. Metal faces of new radiation detection signs
appear next to the crumpled worn idols of stone.
Sunflowers planted in hope, in the names of the dead

fail to purify the earth, say scientists in September.
Still, they are tended. They stand guard with origami cranes
left on the beaches, to be carried away with the tide.

As winter approaches, crushed bodies of cars rest
on rooftops as people try to repair, rebuild. Children's thyroids
tested and scanned. Strontium, cesium, iodine in the soil.
In the fish, the fowl, the fruit.

In the flowers burning in the fields, setting the town alight.

They Do Not Need Rescue

No one needs rescue here in America's Secret City.
Not the robot scientist or his daughter. Not the children
dying of leukemia quietly in hospitals funded
by government grants, uncounted because
their numbers might seem damning.

Not Oak Ridge itself, where the newspaper takes hush
money from ORNL and so mysterious events occur
without any whisper of explanation, where the schools,
churches and highways are built with the largesse of bombs.

In the forest, the hum of generators larger
than you imagine. The fishermen will tell you not to worry
about the catfish. "Gives us a healthy glow,"
they will chuckle. Any complaints stay private.
If you knock on the door and offer help,

they won't know what you're talking about.
They've signed away the lives of their families
on government papers. They do not discuss cancer
at the breakfast table. They might suffer and die,
but they do so in respectable silence.

They do not take kindly to outsiders and advice.
They do not speak of what they, their parents, grandparents
witnessed in Buildings X, Y, or K. Documents warn
of treason for unsealing envelopes, lips. They are truck
drivers, janitors, and yes, sometimes scientists.

They've signed away their rights for a modest paycheck,
for a row of houses starting to crack, and for this,
generations of creeping but unspoken suspicions—

the unsettlement, the slow leak from concrete caps
only now starting to escape.

The Robot Scientist's Daughter [brushes with death]

drowned when she was three.
Her brother was stung to death by wasps.
She died in her sickbed of scarlet fever,
and all her toys and books were burned.

The Robot Scientist's Daughter has become a specter;
she haunts the Children's Hospital wards, plays ball
with the children and hangs their bright pictures
on the wall. She is careful with their IV lines,
their thin fragile skulls.

The Robot Scientist's Daughter spent all of college
with pneumonia, coughing on her exam papers.
She haunts the dorms, pulling fire alarms and shuffling
the carefully stacked pages of the study group.

She died during a routine operation, bled to death
on the table. The hospital lacked facilities for transfusions.
She is a white-faced ghost in an ill-fitting gown,
her feet still in pink slipper socks.

The Robot Scientist's Daughter is amazed she made it
this far. So many brushes with death. That German Shepherd
attack in France, when she jumped into a river; the skittering
puddle-jumper lurching over turbulent Kentucky air.

If she is a ghost, she has no memory. She takes photographs
to remember her home. Images dissolve around her; first
she is holding a television remote, a copy of Cosmo,
her mother's textbooks. The curve of a boy's neck.

The whisper of the afterlife is nothing but frost
on a window; her secrets will die locked
inside her chest, her bones brittle fragments
spelling out her mistakes. Find her among fossils.

Interpreting Signs in Appalachia

In this story, a girl grows up surrounded
by abnormal blooms, pea shoots and peonies.
She learns to ride ponies, goes barefoot
in the treacherous grass. Sickly, she dreams
in the arms of apple trees, spits out their green piths.
It's likely her thyroid grew to the size
of a poisoned apple, that her blood ran hot,
that her hair grew long with trace metals.
It's likely you won't find her happy ending here,
sewn into the silent concrete. Look to the swallows—
they carry their mythic toxins in the walls of their nests,
tucked into nooks, hidden between stones. Search
for clues to the mystery, follow the green light
of foxfire into the sides of mountains, beneath silos.
Listen for the crackle underground.

Notes

To write this book, I spent several years researching the topics here, including reading the transcripts of Town Hall meetings about ORNL workers' health (and the health of their children and grandchildren), EPA papers of the possible contamination and adverse effects of that contamination in Oak Ridge (publicly available, but hard to find and written in very abstruse language) as well as many books, including, probably most helpfully, a fascinating memoir by an early health safety physicist at ORNL called *The Angry Genie*, by Karl Z. Morgan and Ken M. Peterson.

I specifically reference several movies in the manuscript, including *Blade Runner* and the classic (and one of my favorite Mystery Science 3000 episodes), *Killer Shrews*.

Some of the ephemera I consulted were only available briefly online, on people's blogs that have disappeared or government sites that have been re-routed, but some links, as of this writing, still remain available, including:

http://www.epa.gov/region4/superfund/sites/fedfacs/oakridrestn.html

http://www.atsdr.cdc.gov/sites/oakridge/

http://www.atsdr.cdc.gov/toxfaqs/tf.asp?id=576&tid=107

http://energy.gov/iea/downloads/inspection-oak-ridge-national-laboratory-july-2004

http://www.oakridgetn.gov/department/Library/Reference/Books-about-Oak-Ridge

"Cesium Burns Blue": Cesium burns with a blue light. It explodes on contact with water. It also has a highly radioactive isotope which was used in experiments at Oak Ridge. Children ingesting produce grown in contaminated soil might exhibit mental symptoms as well as physical symptoms later in life.

"Hot Wasp Nest": "Wildlife populations have access to some radioactively contaminated sites at Oak Ridge National Laboratory...Mud-dauber wasps (Hymenoptera) and swallows (Hirundinidae) may transport radioactive mud for nest building..."

(From *The Journal of Environmental Radioactivity*, Volume 29, Issue 2, 1995: "Dispersal of radioactivity by wildlife from contaminated sites in a forested landscape."

Sources:

http://www.time.com/time/magazine/article/0,9171,897250,00.html

http://www.sciencedirect.com/science?_ob=ArticleURL&_udi=B6VB2-3YGV42S-4&

"Oak Ridge Tennessee": TLD stands for thermoluminescent dosimeter.

"Women of America's Secret City: 1945": This *Atlantic Monthly* photo feature by Ed Westcott vividly captures life in the early days at ORNL, inspiring at least one poem in the book (and you can check out the threatening signs I mentioned in the Author's Note for yourself): *http://www.theatlantic.com/infocus/2012/06/the-secret-city/100326/*

"Lessons in Poison": A hot particle is a small, highly radioactive object, with significant content of radionuclides. Most hot particles released into the environment originate in nuclear reactors. They also are a component of the fallout from a nuclear weapon detonation.

"America Dreams of Roswell": The "famous" lizard refers to William Stafford's poem, "At the Bomb Testing Site."

"The Scientist" is dedicated to Karl Ziegler Morgan, a health physicist at Oak Ridge.

"A Morning of Sunflowers": Source of quotations: *http://www.msnbc.msn.com/id/44206319/ns/technology_and_science-science/*

"Tickling the Dragon," after Auden's "Musée Des Beaux Arts," is dedicated to Louis Slotin, who died from acute radiation syndrome after an accident involving nuclear fission. I also reference "Dr. Manhattan," a comic book character from *The Watchmen*, who experienced odd side effects from a similar nuclear accident.

Special Thanks

I would like to say thank you to all the people who gave me valuable feedback and encouragement while I was writing this book. Special thanks to: Kelli Russell Agodon, Lana Hechtman Ayers, Annette Spaulding-Convy, Kelly Davio, Natasha K. Moni, Jenifer Lawrence, Holly Hughes, Janet Knox and Ronda Broatch.

Thanks to Dana Levin for her invaluable advice on earlier versions of this manuscript.

Thanks to Kaori Yoshida, Kumiko Onoda and Yorifumi Yaguchi who translated some of this work into Japanese for the bilingual anthology, *Farewell to Nuclear, Welcome to Renewable Energy*.

I would like to thank my wonderful editors at Mayapple Press, Judith Kerman and Amee Schmidt.

I would like to thank artist Masaaki Sasamoto for creating and allowing us to use the amazing cover art (from his "Cocoro" series) for this book.

Thanks to Tom Collicott for his work on the author photo.

Thanks to the authors of *The Angry Genie: One Man's Walk Through the Nuclear Age*, Karl Ziegler Morgan and Ken M. Peterson, for information about the early days of Oak Ridge National Labs.

Many thanks to the Dorothy Sargent Rosenberg Prize for giving me the financial support I needed to work on this manuscript.

And thanks to my husband Glenn Allen Gailey and to my family for their support.

About the Author

Jeannine Hall Gailey recently served as the Poet Laureate of Redmond, Washington, and is the author of three other books of poetry: *Unexplained Fevers, She Returns to the Floating World* and *Becoming the Villainess.* Her work has been featured on NPR's *Writer's Almanac, Verse Daily* and was included in *The Year's Best Horror.* Her poems have appeared *The American Poetry Review, The Iowa Review,* and *Prairie Schooner.* Her web site is *www.webbish6. com.*

Other Recent Titles from Mayapple Press:

Carlo Matos, *The Secret Correspondence of Loon and Fiasco*, 2014
> Paper, 110pp, $16.95 plus s&h
> ISBN 978-1-936419-46-3

Chris Green, *Resumé*, 2014
> Paper, 72pp, $15.95 plus s&h
> ISBN 978-1-936419-44-9

Paul Nemser, Tales of the Tetragrammaton, 2014
> Paper, 34pp, $12.95 plus s&h
> ISBN 978-1-936419-43-2

Catherine Anderson, *Woman with a Gambling Mania*, 2014
> Paper, 72pp, $15.95 plus s&h
> ISBN 978-1-936419-41-8

Victoria Fish, *A Brief Moment of Weightlessness*, 2014
> Paper, 132pp, $16.95 plus s&h
> ISBN 978-1-936419-40-1

Susana H. Case, *4 Rms w Vu*, 2014
> Paper, 72pp, $15.95 plus s&h
> ISBN 978-1-936419-39-5

Elizabeth Genovise, *A Different Harbor*, 2014
> Paper, 76pp, $15.95 plus s&h
> ISBN 978-1-936419-38-8

Marjorie Stelmach, *Without Angels*, 2014
> Paper, 74pp, $15.95 plus s&h
> ISBN 978-1-936419-37-1

David Lunde, *The Grandson of Heinrich Schliemann & Other Truths and Fictions*, 2014
> Paper, 62pp, $14.95 plus s&h
> ISBN 978-1-936419-36-4

Eleanor Lerman, *Strange Life*, 2014
> Paper, 90pp, $15.95 plus s&h
> ISBN 978-1-936419-35-7

Sally Rosen Kindred, *Book of Asters*, 2014
> Paper, 74pp, $15.95 plus s&h
> ISBN 978-1-936419-34-0

For a complete catalog of Mayapple Press publications, please visit our website at *www.mayapplepress.com*. Books can be ordered direct from our website with secure on-line payment using PayPal, or by mail (check or money order). Or order through your local bookseller.